New Creative Print Making

New Creative Print Making

Peter Green

WATSON-GUPTILL PUBLICATIONS
NEW YORK

Published MCMLXIV by B.T. Batsford Limited, London
Published MCMLXV by Watson-Guptill Publications, New York, New York 10036
Reprinted MCMLXVI

Printed and bound in Denmark by F.E. Bording Limited, Copenhagen and London
Library of Congress Catalog Card Number 65-21692

8518

Contents

Acknowledgment

The majority of prints in this book are the work of young students, from Secondary schools, attending Saturday morning classes at the Hornsey College of Art.

For permission to use this work my thanks are due to the Principal Mr H. H. Shelton, ARCA, ARE, FSAE, ASIA (Ed.), NRD. These classes are run by the Department of Teacher Training and many of the other prints are the work of students in this Department. I would therefore like to thank the staff and students of the Department, and Mr James Townley, ARE, ATD, now Head of the Department of Fine Art, Sheffield College of Art.

A large number of students and colleagues have been concerned in the printing projects which appear in this book. I am grateful for all their help and especially to Mr Kim Kempshall, ARCA, at present lecturer in charge of print making at Edinburgh College of Art, who began with me the initial printing project at Hornsey, and without whose energy much of the work would not have developed.

Among the many other friends, I would like to thank Jon Tacey, John Hegarty and George Large; Douglas Lowndes for taking all the photographs; Miss Thelma M. Nye of B.T. Batsford Ltd, who has patiently given a great deal of advice and help, and finally, Mr Maurice Barrett, Art Adviser for the London Borough of Redbridge and Barking, who with many others, has helped by so willingly lending me work.

London 1964   *P. G.*

Introduction

This book is concerned with the fundamental nature of surfaces and creative print making using simple processes with basic materials.

The methods shown deal with relief printing in which the raised part of the surface, the *printing image,* is inked and transferred onto paper. Little pressure is needed and all the examples have been produced without a printing press.

The beginnings of print making lie in the simple awareness of surface—rough or smooth, fine or coarse. When ink is rolled evenly over any surface and paper pressed onto the 'inked up' surface it will reveal the nature of that surface on paper.

Printing a surface can be a process of discovery, in which we are curious about the quality of a surface and by printing it discover its visual nature. We begin to see through a sense of touch, as in braille, and this 'seeing' becomes visual when printed.

It should be emphasised that the work in this book is not primarily concerned with the production of works of art or with the practice and acquisition of particular techniques or skills, and as such should not be considered as a separate craft activity. So many crafts have their special secret skills and are contained in separate compartments which so often prove barriers to learning and expression.

Print making here is not an end in itself but is used as a method through which the young person may develop his visual and tactile knowledge. What is encouraged is a willingness to explore materials creatively. The so called 'work of Art' will emerge naturally as a by-product.

1 Rubbings and direct prints of surfaces

Rubbing with a crayon is the simplest and most direct form of printing, and the exact quality and texture of any surface is made apparent by this process.

This not only helps in understanding the fundamental principle of relief print making but also in developing an awareness of the surfaces to be found around us.

Making a rubbing demands no specific skill, just a little care. It can, however, help dispel the mystery so often attached to making a printing block and can illustrate clearly how the difference in height of layers of any particular surface will allow the raised parts to the printed.

Direct prints of surfaces can be made either by inking up the surface and pressing paper onto it or by the offset method which is especially useful with delicate materials (see pages 115 and 120).

The first series of rubbings and direct prints are from natural surfaces, leaves, feathers, wood and other materials. Such prints not only illustrate the simple principle of relief printing but also make us more aware of the nature and character of each particular surface or form. The capacity of such prints to develop perception through such visual evidence is important. What is learnt at this stage about textures not only opens our eyes but can help show the range of surfaces that can possibly be created in the students' own prints.

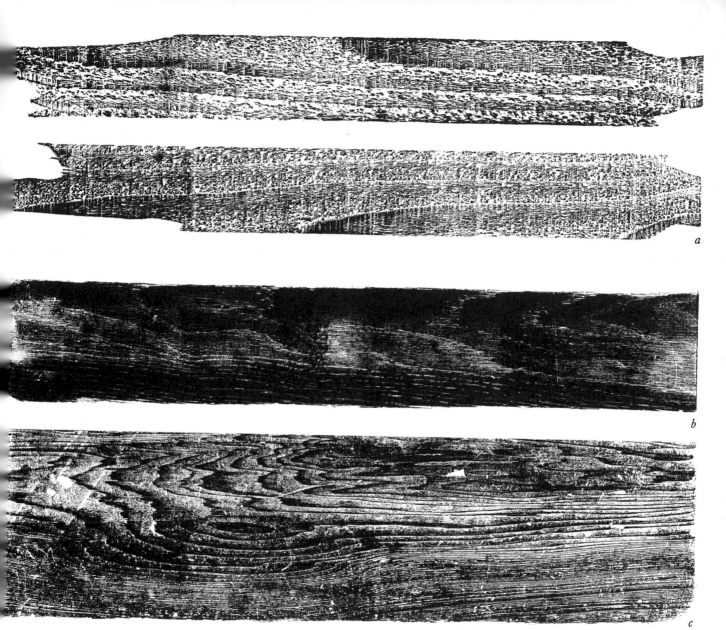

a Both sides of a piece of drift-wood with the grain pronounced by the effects of sea water

b Hardwood, printed with a hard roller so that the fine grain does not fill in with ink

c Scrubbed wood. A wire brush can be used to remove softer parts of wood and emphasise the grain

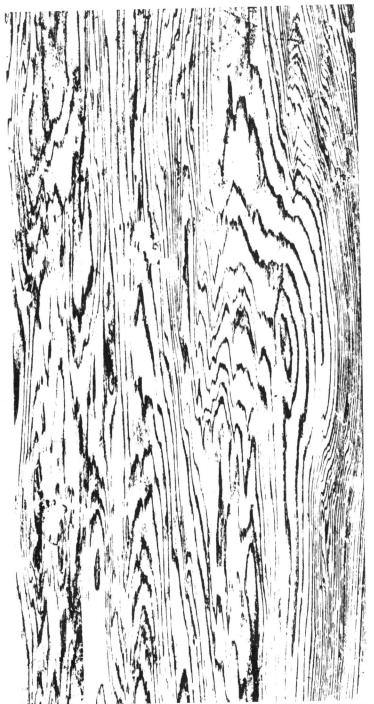

a

b

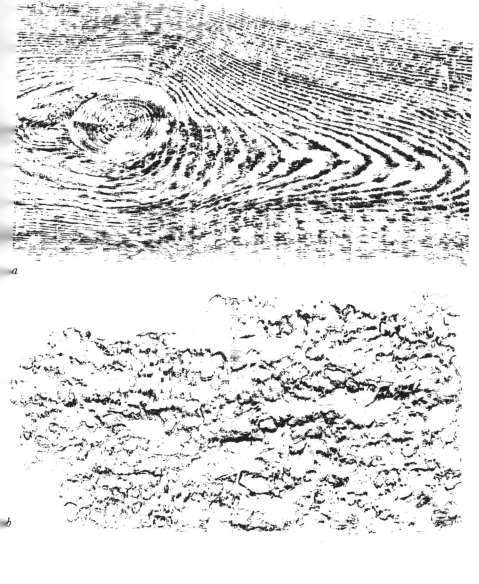

Opposite

a Rubbing of scrubbed wood surface

b Print of thin plywood sheet

Crayon rubbings of wood surfaces

a Plank grain

b Bark

c Showing grain and saw marks

Offset prints of feathers

This method of printing is ideal for fine textures (see pages 115 and 120)

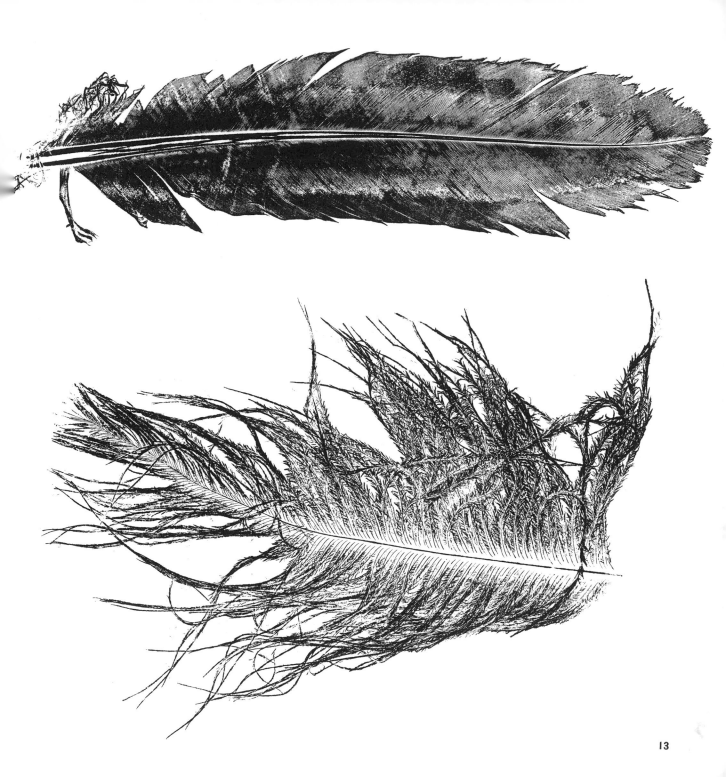

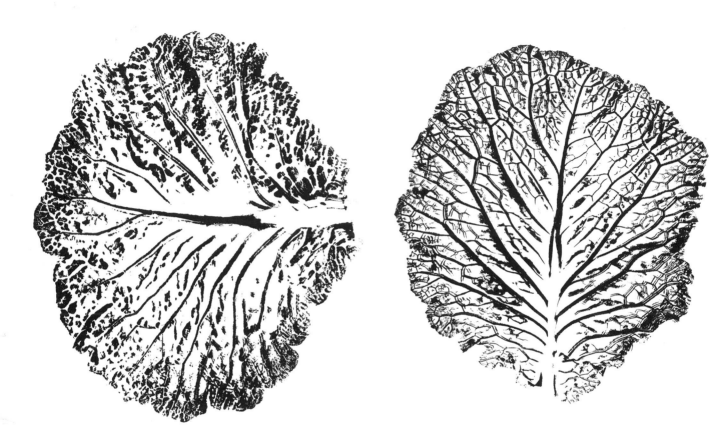

Direct prints of cabbage leaves showing a well defined relief surface

Offset prints of leaves

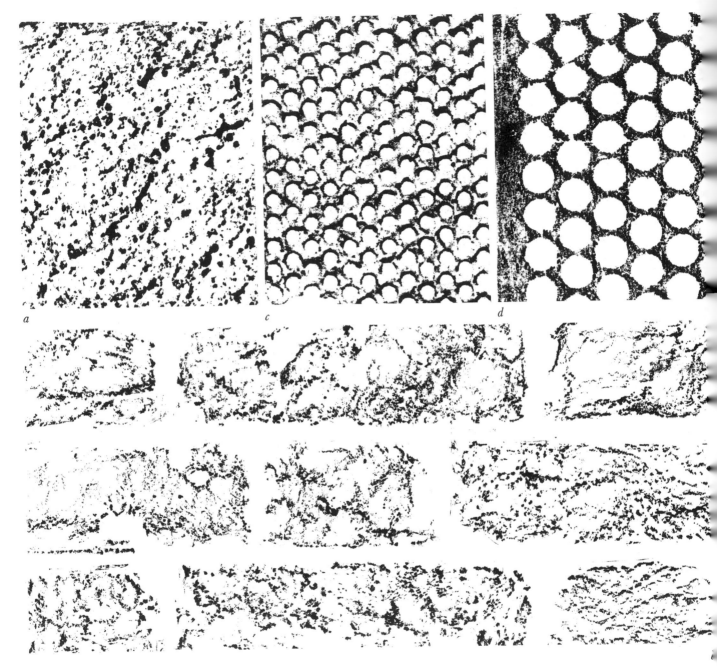

Crayon rubbings of rough surfaces

a and b Stone and brick. Quality of surface
not apparent until 'printed'

c Asbestos sheet
d Perforated tile

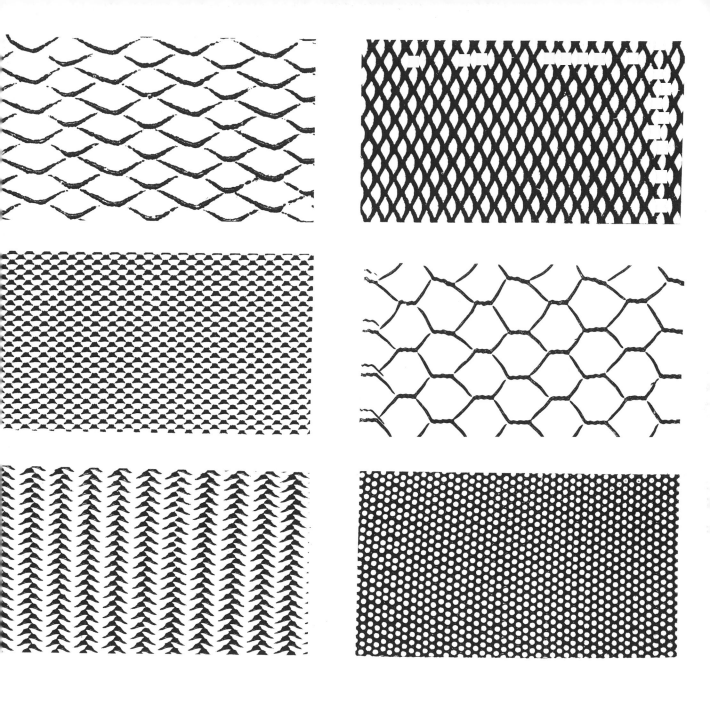

nts from a variety of wire and metal mesh sheets

19

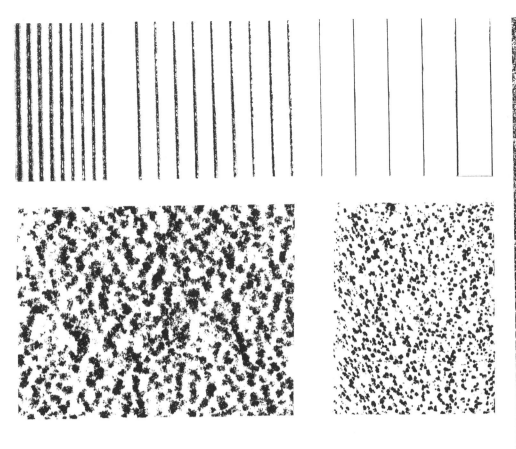

Crayon rubbings of patterned glass

Opposite

a Piece of glass printed with a hard roller, revealing only the top surface of ridges

b The same piece printed with a soft roller, allowing the ink to print the lower sections in between the lines

c Patterned glass printed both sides
One side has a clearly defined surface, the other a more gradual change in level

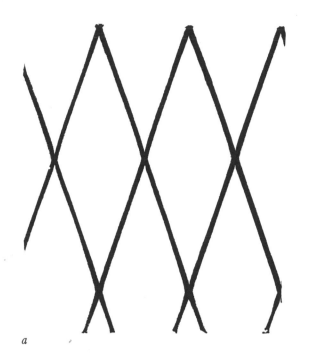

a

b

c

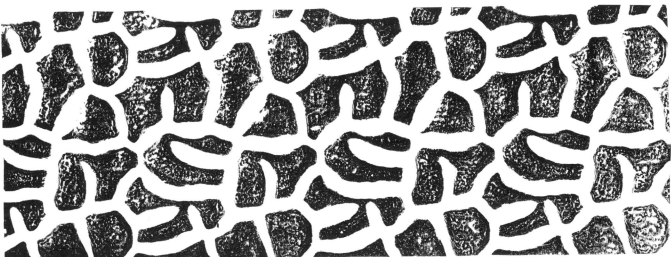

Print of both sides of a piece of patterned glass
The linear pattern is not really evident until printed

Opposite   Prints of cloth and fabrics   *a*   Corduroy

b   Fine net

c   Dish cloth

d   Lace

e   Sacking

a

b

c

d

e

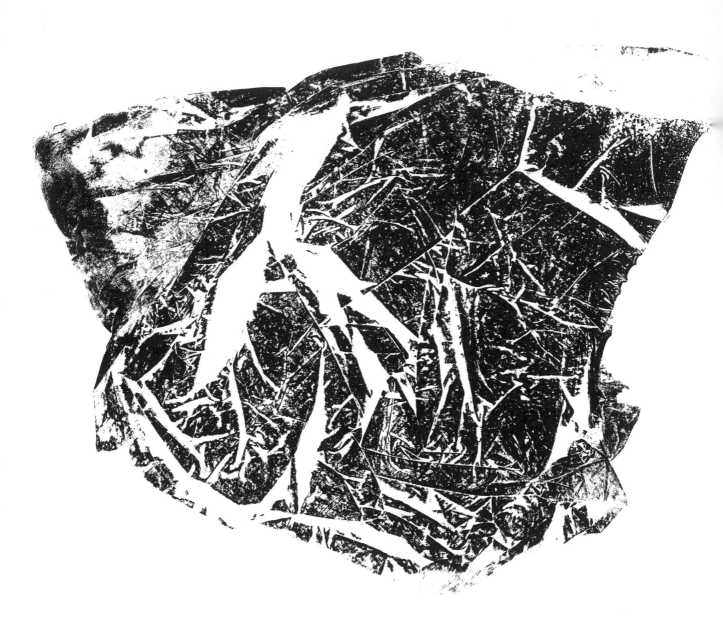

Crinkled paper

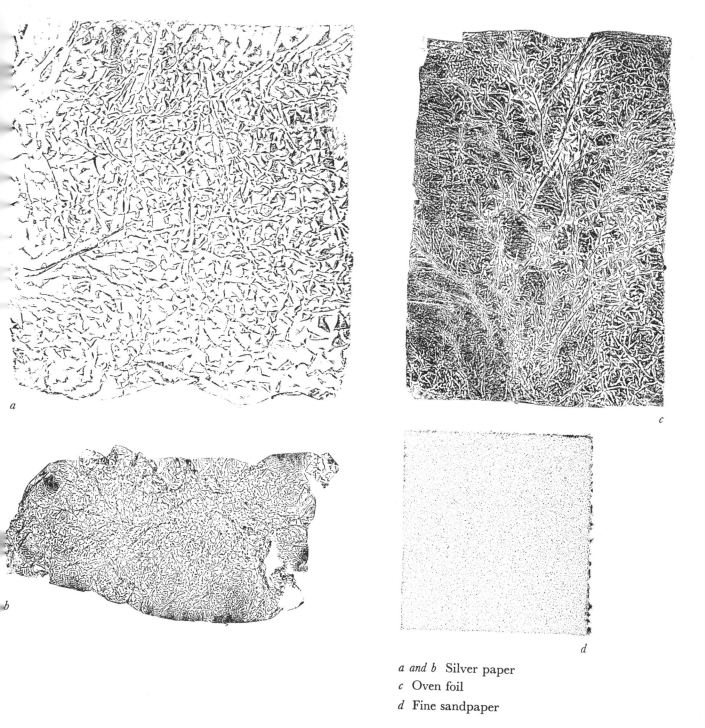

a

b

c

d

a and b Silver paper
c Oven foil
d Fine sandpaper

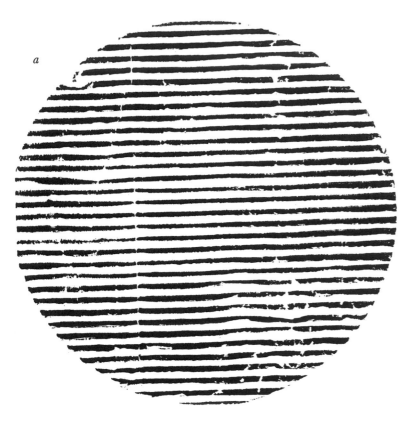

a

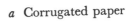

a Corrugated paper

b Textured wrapping paper from chocolate boxes

c Section of crinkled paper from fruit box wrapping

b

2 Collecting surfaces and building up images

In this section the process of searching into the qualities of surfaces and texture is developed.

Materials and actual surfaces are collected and stuck down onto a board, usually hardboard, either with impact glue or by nailing. (A sheet of stiff paper is suitable.)

What has been learnt about surfaces is used in selecting various materials and textures and arranging them in relation to each other to form an image. In these exercises the emphasis is not on how one draws but on developing the capacity to make a rational decision as to *where* a piece of material is placed and the shape it should take: its shape being defined by cutting or tearing it, which is in fact 'drawing'.

The block is then inked up, taking care not to pick up any loose pieces of material, paper is placed over the inked block and a proof taken by pressing the paper onto the block (see pages 114 and 117).

The best prints are often taken when the first film of ink on the block has dried and soaked into the surface. Materials are very often too absorbent and the ink tends to sink in leaving little ink to be transferred to the paper, thus producing a very pale print. If, however, the ink has been allowed to dry on the surface a little, by the time the second print is taken it will seal the block and also help to fix any loose pieces onto the board.

In building up the block too great a difference in the height or thickness of various materials should be avoided. Although all the various materials need not be of a standard height, too great a difference obviously brings difficulty in both inking up the block and in pressing the paper onto it.

Once the paper is laid onto the inked surface care should be taken that it does not move. One hand should always keep the paper still while the other is used for pressing.

As in all this work the object is not to produce beautiful pictures or 'works of Art' but to explore a variety of materials and textures; to arrange these in relation to each other and to organise these elements within a given rectangle. The interesting image is a by-product of this process.

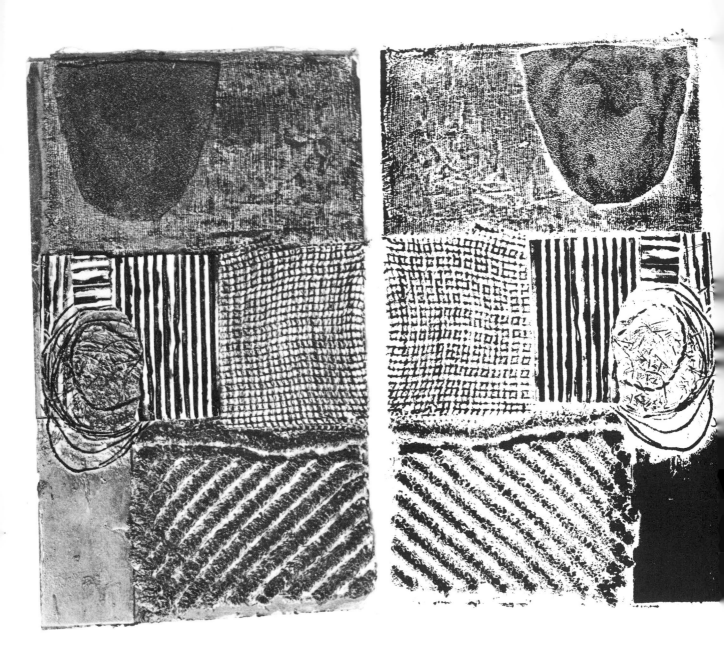

Block and print

Well organised solution to problem of arranging
various shapes and textures within a given rectangle

The emphasis is placed on achieving visual order
which would be destroyed if any part were taken
away or anything added

Collage prints by 9-year-old children
Imaginative pictorial use of scraps of strawboard,
metal mesh, string and scraps of wood

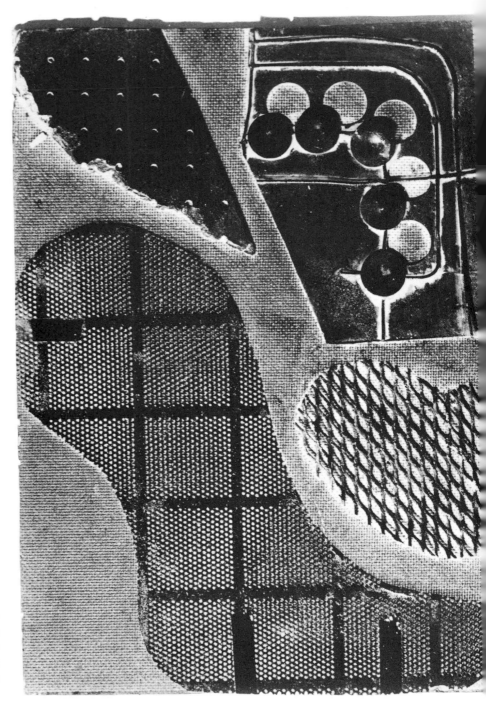

Block and print

Metal mesh, perforated hardboard and scrap metal stuck onto hardboard. Texture of hardboard base also printed. The shapes are considered carefully and are drawn and well defined by cutting with scissors

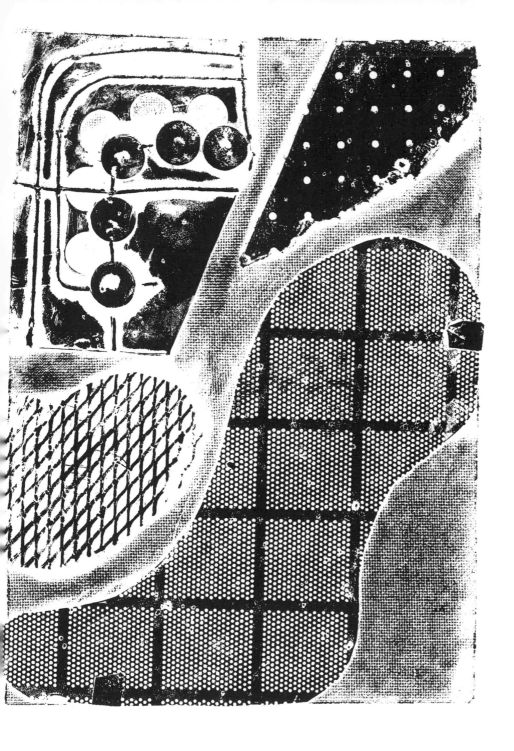

Block and print showing the use of plasterboard, metal mesh asbestos, perforated hardboard, plastic grid, corrugated card

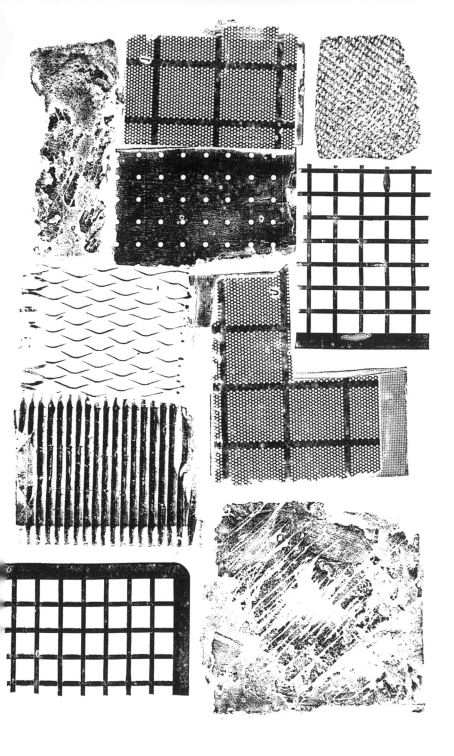

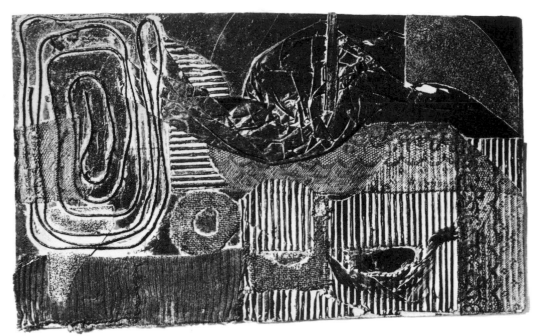

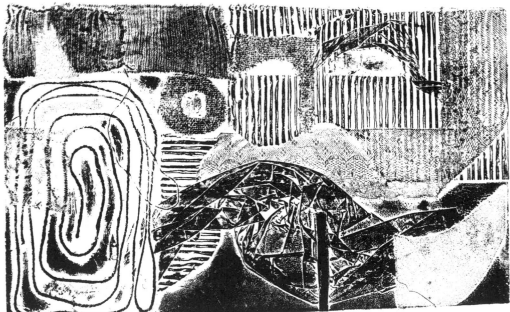

Block and Print
Crinkled paper, string, sandpaper, lace cloth and
corrugated card all carefully controlled and exploited to form an imaginative image

Collage prints from collected surfaces
stuck onto board

a

a Print using sand and cut card shapes
Glue painted onto the base board; sand and grit sprinkled over this while wet, creating a relief surface which is printed when dry

Opposite

b Metal mesh, string and wire
The white 'halo' around the metal shape is formed by the raised edge between the base board and the metal shape which does not receive the ink

c Fantasy figure collage
Imaginative use of Sellotape, which fulfils the function of holding the string in position while at the same time forming an important visual part of the printed design

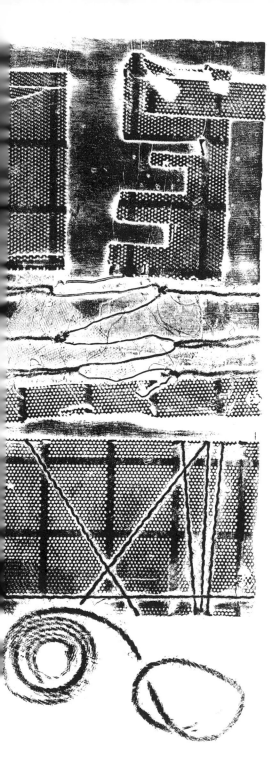

c

Collage of metal shapes on hardboard

3   Cutting into a material

We have seen how a print can be made by building up a surface, sticking down materials and printing from the raised parts; the next stage deals with cutting into a material. When a cut is made the surface of the material becomes the printing surface and the cut parts, being lower, remain white.

In this section the aim is to explore the kind of marks and incisions possible in all types of materials and to develop the realisation that the white mark made by cutting is simply another form of drawing. Soft materials can be dented or pressed into. Harder materials have to be cut, scratched or hammered.

No rigid emphasis is put on the way a cut is made. Method is determined by the result required and an understanding of the nature of both material and tool.

Hardboard, a comparatively cheap material, can be scratched into with a nail or any sharp point and an immediate printing line made. It cuts well with a knife and the surface can also be torn, giving a softer edge. Strawboard, balsa wood and other soft materials do not necessarily need to be cut into. A printing surface can be made by simply pressing into them. One of the advantages of this method is that an object, texture or pattern can be transferred directly by being pressed into the soft material.

Experiments should be encouraged with different materials and an analysis made of the variety of cut line and texture that each surface naturally produces. Some materials can be cut easily, others are best engraved, and some scored or torn. Plywood and veneer board can be drawn into with scratched or cut line giving a crisp clean result, and the layers of plywood can be split away to create varying printing layers. Lino is an easy material to cut. It is without grain, soft and even in texture and capable of being worked into in a great variety of ways. The plank grain of wood is ideal material. Selected for its grain and salvaged from all manner of sources it can have a considerable potential. The grain should be accepted as an inherent part of the print, and used to create an image that depends on it. This is best done by printing the uncut wood first, examining the nature of the surface and letting this be the starting point.

Special tools need not be bought for cutting into many of these materials. A sharp knife can well be a basic tool, and any tool or improvised object can be used, though a broader chisel is useful for cleaning out larger areas.

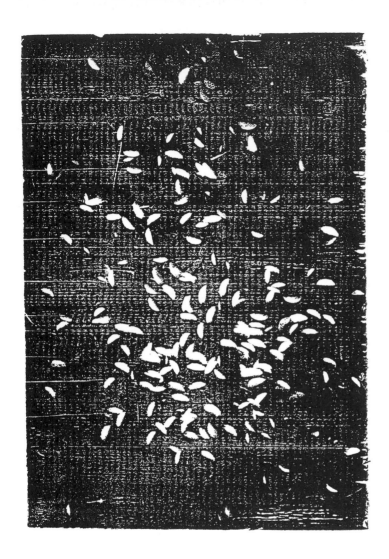

A block does not have to be cut with special tools —marks and images can be made in all sorts of ways, as this hammered piece of wood by a 2-year-old boy clearly shows

a

b

ardboard cuts

showing crisp quality of line

showing contrast between cut and scratched line

a

a Chipboard cut with a knife. Cuts easily and has
a surface texture which allows the black parts to
remain fairly open and grey

b Shapes cut out of the side of a wooden box
Use of lettering already on wood and rich texture
of cut marks

Hardboard cut

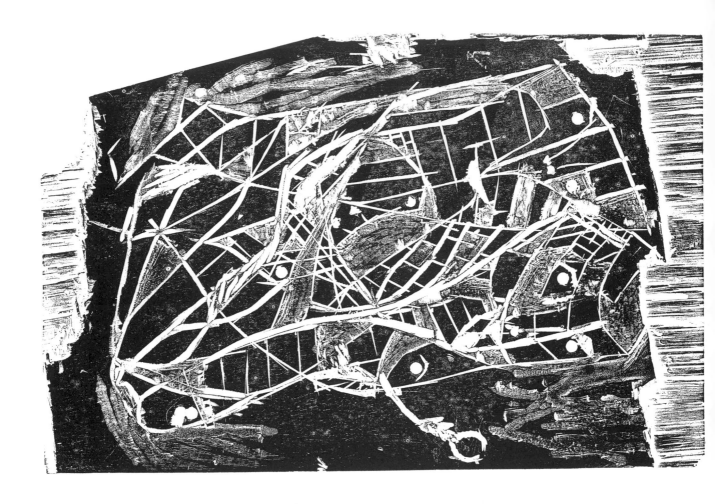

Scrap plywood
Around the edge of the print can be seen where a
layer of ply has been pulled off and a lower layer
printed

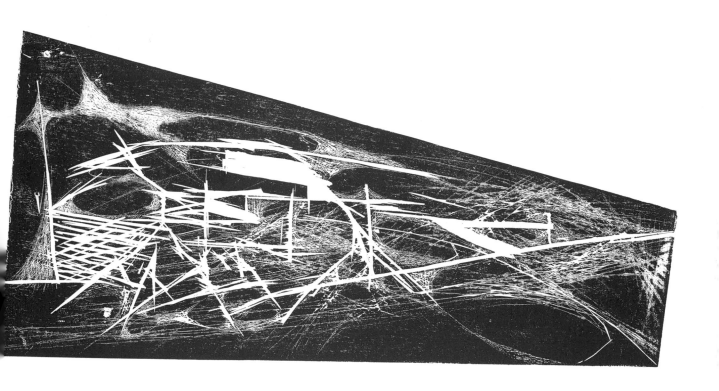

Veneer wood
Hard surface which has been scratched into with
the point of a knife and nail

a

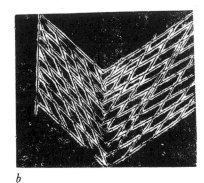

b

c

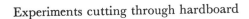

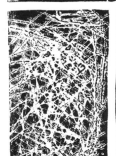

d

Experiments cutting through hardboard

a Top layer of hardboard pulled off leaving a softer texture below to be printed

b Scratched line creates a burr or ridge which can actually produce a black line on white. This burr can easily be removed with a spatula or the edge of a palette knife or can be left as a black line

c Examples of cut line, scratched line and hammered textures with nail point

d Further examples of experimental cuts

Hardboard cut

a Scrap of hard varnished plywood scratched point of compass

b Woodcut. Cut marks influenced by knot grain of wood

Hardboard prints

a Printing the lower surface and revealing the natural pattern of tool marks

b Using a hard roller and leaving the areas that have been cut away clean and white
The tool marks made naturally in clearing an area have been exploited in these illustrations. This is pattern as a natural by-product of the way of working with the tool and material

b

Soft display board cut with knife and round gouge. This absorbs a great deal of ink when first printed but once ink has dried the surface is sealed and the block prints easily. The block could be sized before printing

Soft board
Good example of pattern growing naturally from cutting away areas and printing the tool marks

...te cuts and scratches easily. Layers tend to ...ke off giving a variety of tone

Paint on the surface of this scrap of wood has been burnt and the resulting texture printed

a

b

c

d

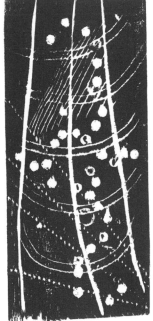

e

f

Balsa wood prints in which objects are pressed directly into the soft surface of the block

a Soft broad marks made with thumb nail, bone folder and the back of a cutting tool

b Nail file, scissors, knife handle and coins

c Lines made with string pressed into block

d Drawing with comb

e and f Examples of the clarity of line possible

sa wood prints

cutting. Impressions made with pencil, circular
, tool handles and other objects

53

a

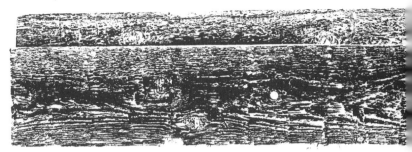

a Hardboard scratched with nail and point of compass

b and c Plank grain woodcut
Wood first printed and nature of grain studied with its resulting influence on the finished print

4   Combining cutting and building up of blocks

In this section prints are made by combining, on the same block, the cut line with areas of built up material and texture. Materials are stuck onto the block and the block itself is also cut into.

When, on the same block, areas are built up and also cut away, the depth of the block that has to be printed can be considerable. Ink has to be placed on the top of the block, the built up areas, and the lower cut areas also need inking.

A soft roller, which can be pressed into the lower areas, is used to ink the block thoroughly and when the paper is placed on the block it needs also to be pressed with something soft, to make sure that the paper is pushed down into the lower parts. This can be done with a soft roller, a soft pad of rag, a layer of sponge or more directly the paper can be pressed down into the block with careful hand pressure. This freedom of printing without a press can be controlled so that a series of identical prints can be obtained.

Block and print
Block with a variety of heights and materials; hen
wire, metal plates and fine net. White lines achieved
by cutting into the hardboard base

Cut block with some areas of tone formed by sticking hessian onto block

Imaginative flower. White line cut into block, other 'petals' and shapes of lace and coconut shell hair stuck on

Hessian and pieces of cut hardboard stuck onto board to form composite block with engraved line

Above   Wire and cloth stuck onto cut block

Opposite   Strange Tree
Stem and branches made of strips of strawboard.
Cut areas, with additional crinkled paper, corru-
gated card and hessian. Printed in two colours

5   Exercise using a single material

The simple printing principles of either building up a surface or cutting down into a material to create an image are now explored in more detail.

From the following exercises is learnt something of the nature of such things as line and tone, shape and colour, texture and pattern. The important thing is not the material and method being used but what is learnt by using it.

An exercise with a single material is used to discover some of the fundamental elements that go to make up visual images and the activity of print making is applied to learn something of the basic language.

All these methods are direct and results can be achieved quite quickly. The methods are not combined or complicated. Each print explores one material only, or one aspect of it. An idea or exercise is set as a problem for each print and the purpose is to solve the problem within the limits of the material chosen.

The prints in this section are arranged in three broad sections; (1) those prints concerned with tone and texture, (2) line and movement, (3) shape and colour. Such classification is inaccurate and limiting, but by separating elements or breaking them down, they can be examined without other considerations interrupting. Indeed such prints may well be exercises only, but they are expressive exercises, in which the potential of a single material is exploited.

Two hardboard cuts with a number of objects
drawn directly onto the block with a cutting tool

Tone and texture exercise
Solve the problem of defining the shape of each
object without using a rigid outline

Corrugated card

Easily available in large quantities and free
Excellent for tonal exercises of this kind
The top surface a full black when printed. The
middle ridges, exposed by peeling off the top layer,
give a regular half tone
The white is achieved by cutting right through the
corrugated sandwich

Corrugated card

...onal exercise used to achieve the effect of recession
...nd depth

Free shapes cut into corrugated card, breaking away deliberately from the rectangular quality

In most of the exercises in this book the young person is not learning with a visual aid showing him what to do and solving the problem for him. He is learning by trying to solve a series of problems which are set him. These are enforced experiences so disciplined that there is no way round other than by learning and experiencing, and completing the task using imagination and rational thought. The following exercise, which illustrates this approach, is aimed to develop an understanding of the use of texture and tone

Four identical shapes if printed either touching each other or overlapping could not retain the identity of their individual shape if printed in the same colour

Problem
By using only one colour make each shape 'read' individually when printed partially overlapping and using only one colour
The rules must be observed, for it is only by such discipline that the valid solution can be worked out

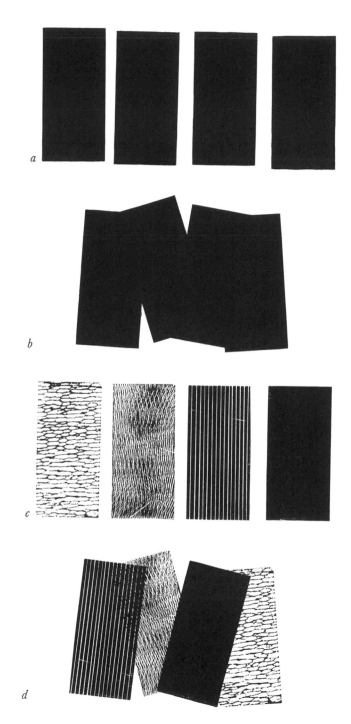

a Four identical pieces of lino

b The four printed overlapping, illustrating how the individual shape disappears

c Breaking down the tone value of each rectangle by cutting into lino
Colour could not be used and the student was forced to develop his understanding of texture and tone by the necessity of solving a clearly set problem

d The four shapes printed as in stage *b*

a

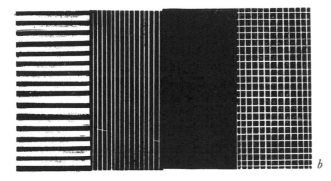

b

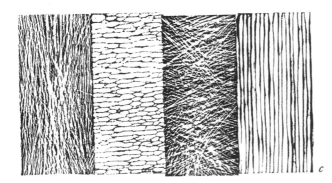

c

d

Further examples of the exercise illustrated on page 67, in which four identical rectangles of lino are used

a Four shapes printed edge to edge forming large rectangle. Identity of individual rectangle disappears

b Individual rectangles appearing clearly defined although printed touching each other. Tone broken down using only straight lines

c Solution using freer textures

d Spacial achievement. One shape appearing in front of the other

Problem
Using the same colour overprint the shape to achieve a sense of depth

Perforated hardboard. *Tone exercise*. The whole
block printed in black but a variety of 'greys'
achieved by use of perforated patterns breaking
down the power, or visual value of the black
In addition to various perforated pieces of hardboard the back of the hardboard is also used
This gives a further variation and shows how tints
and tonal 'colour' can be achieved

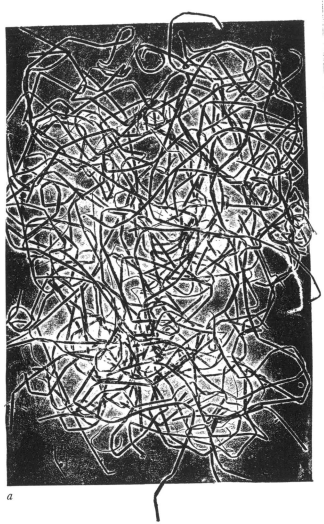

a

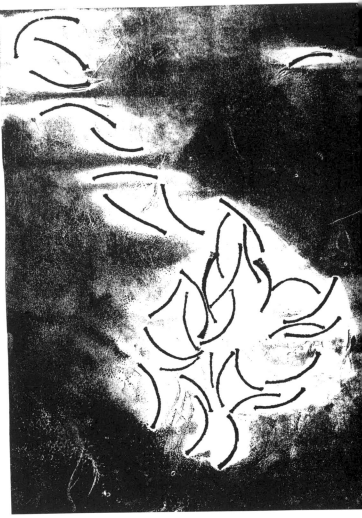

The exercises on the following pages are concerned with printing and exploring certain materials illustrating the quality and use of line

a Wood wool stuck onto paper and printed

b A set number of similar length pieces of string pasted onto paper, achieving a sense of movement without being joined together into a continuous line

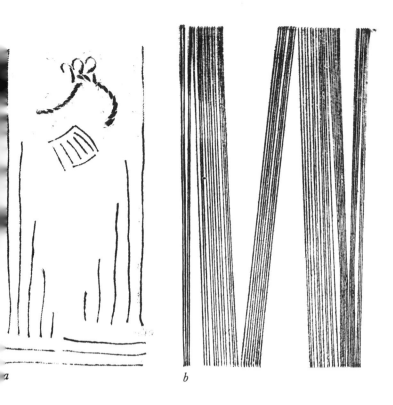

a

b

c

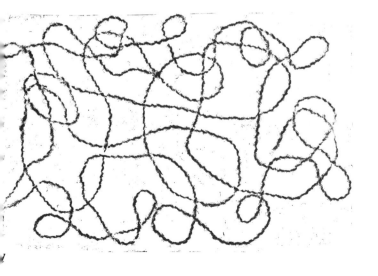

d

a String on paper. Static design printed with a hard roller. Only the ridges of string print and the background is left white

b Parallel lines of string. A single length of string wound around a piece of board. Variations in the arrangement of lines can be achieved by moving the string along the edges of the board

c Free exploration of linear quality of string again printing only the top ridges

d Print from wool stuck onto paper

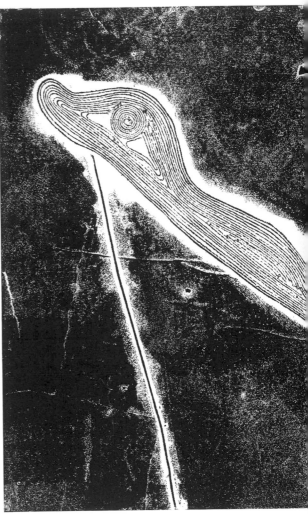

String print. Inking up the whole block including the background leaving the white halo around the edge of the string where the roller cannot penetrate

Exploiting the fact that string comes in a ball and tends naturally to take on a curved quality when placed on paper

a

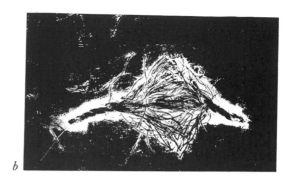

b

c

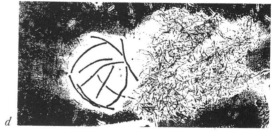

d

a String print aiming to divide the rectangle into various areas

b String opened out

c Plaited string

d String chopped up and dropped onto glued paper

73

Various examples of prints from matchsticks
A readily available printing material giving an
opportunity to build up a linear image with units
of the same length

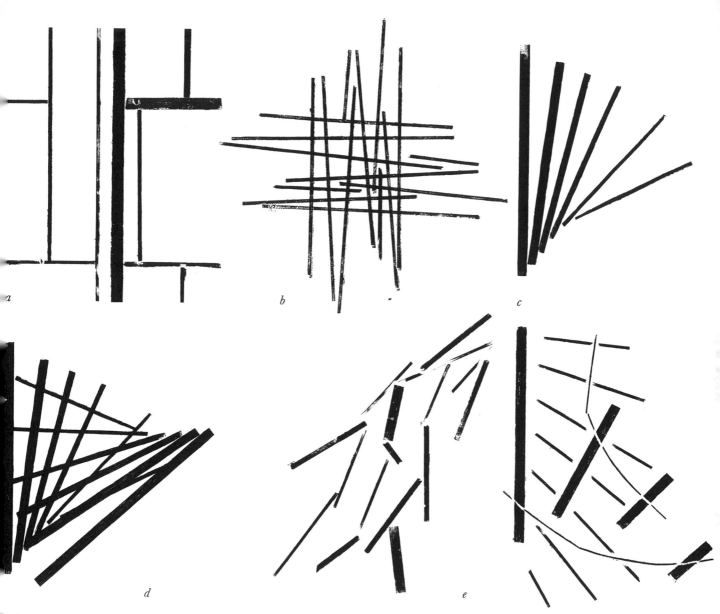

Balsa wood stick prints—balsa sticks stuck onto paper and printed

a Division of area using straight lines and maintaining right angles

b A simpler linear block overprinted in opposite directions

c Six lines arranged to achieve sense of movement

d The same block printed twice, as in *b*

e Two examples expressing sense of linear movement

Some sticks cut thinly to produce curved lines

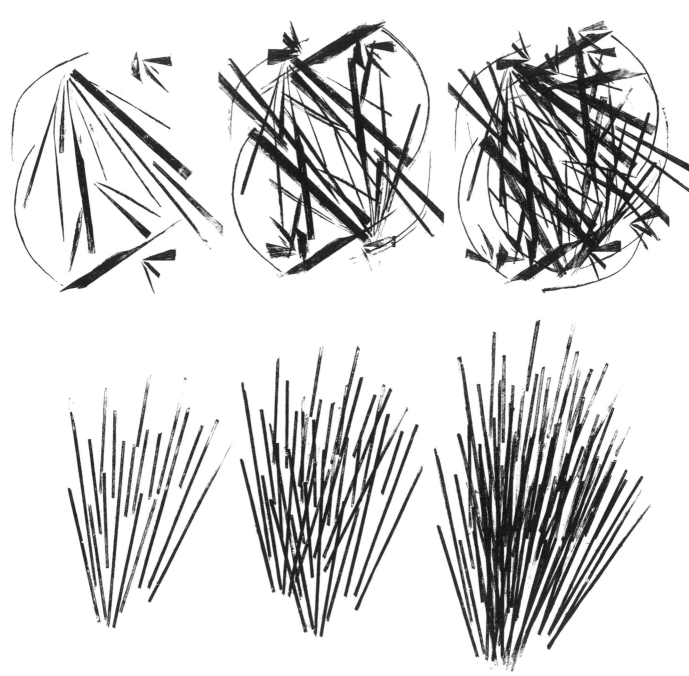

Two linear exercises in balsa wood sticks overprinted
progressively to develop an idea

76

A sheet of corrugated card when printed forms a field of parallel lines. Circles cut out of the card and turned round alter the direction of lines

a Exercise in line to explore the visual effect of moving certain lines
Eight circles are cut out and parallel direction of lines change. This is an experiment in using line to achieve sense of depth, space and movement

b Different result with same block
Three circles removed, giving white and further sense of depth
Four circles moved with lines at right angle to background giving visual appearance of bringing them forward

c Further experiment with the same block, using overprinting of lines and cutting further circles within original circles

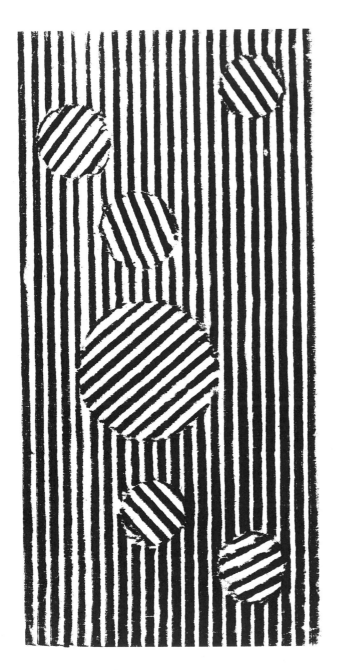

Corrugated card

Exercise in linear movement and illusion of space

Overprinting the same block in opposite directions
Exploring the variety and nature of the 'negative'
white shapes in between lines

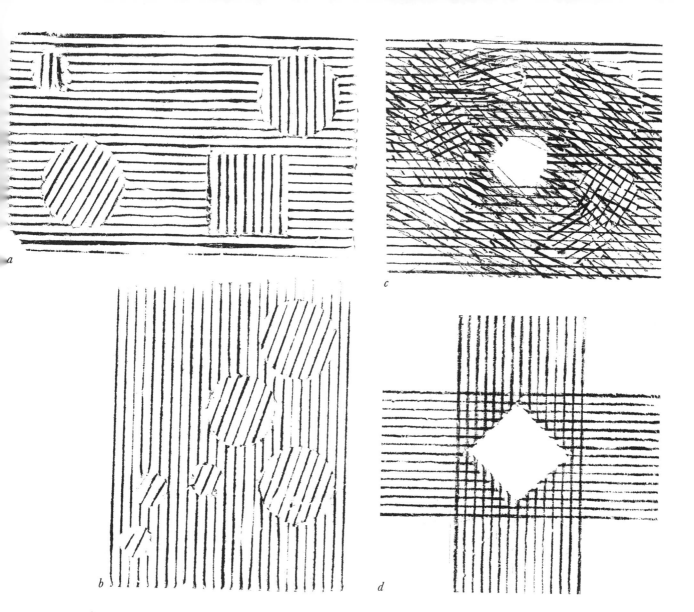

a and b Corrugated card
Circles and square cut out and replaced, altering
the static background of lines

c Overprinting corrugated block several times in
various directions

d Simple corrugated block overprinted at right
angles
Exercise, as in *(c)*, of building up contrast of tone
with overprinted lines

Further experiments with overprinted corrugated
card blocks

a

b

c

d

a A series of squares cut out inside a larger square
The linear direction of each square alternated

b Series of squares and circles within each other,
with the final small circle overprinted

c Series of rings cut from a circle of corrugated
card, printed together
Each ring twisted round away from the original
parallel lines

d Corrugated card spiral

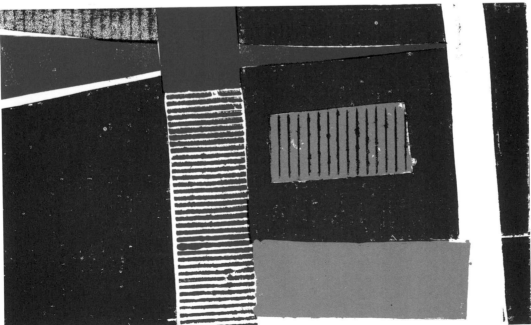

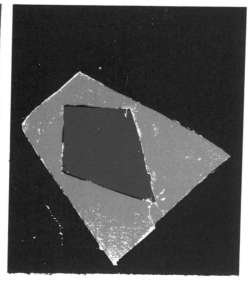

Colour corrugated card prints

A method in which many colours can be printed at the same time Shapes are cut out of the cardboard, inked up in various colours then slotted back and printed all at the same time

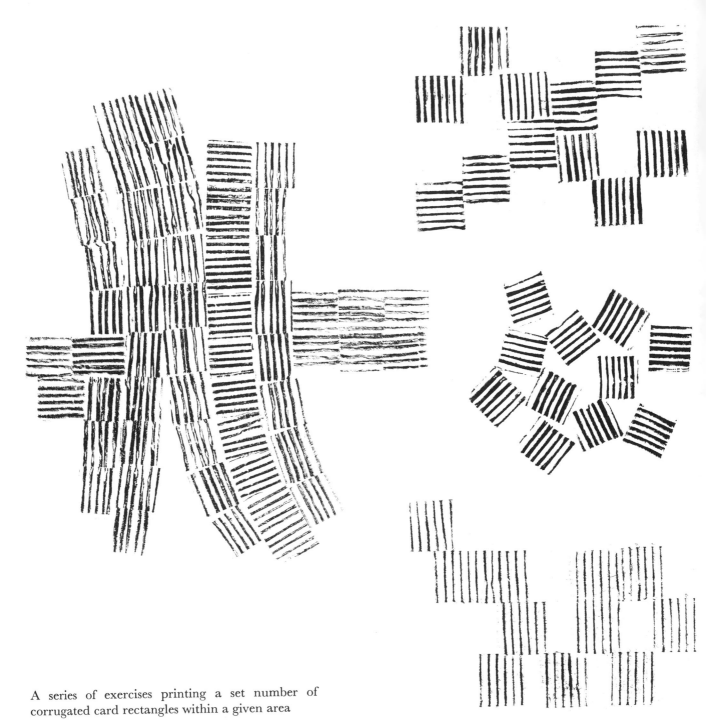

A series of exercises printing a set number of
corrugated card rectangles within a given area

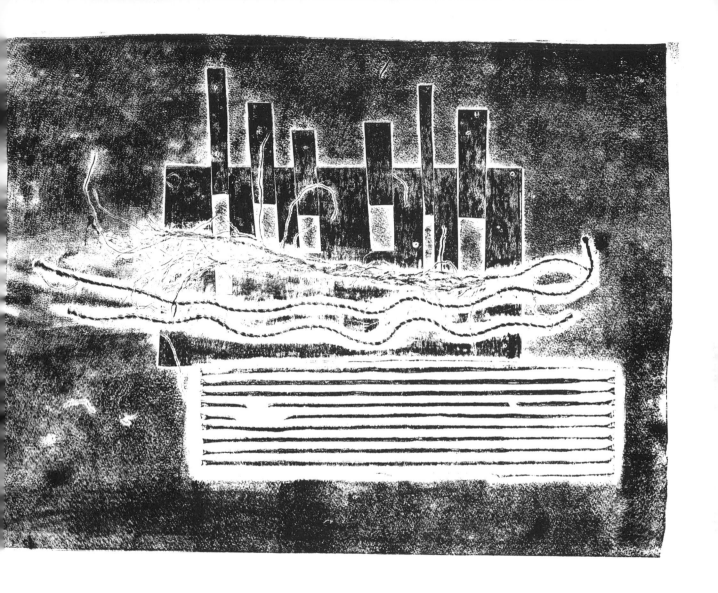

A combined block contrasting the linear character
of corrugated card, string and paper

Sellotape prints. Sellotape stuck onto wood (Scotch tape or adhesive tape of other types could be used)
Building up the Sellotape, printing the block at progressive stages
The smooth surface of the Sellotape prints against the texture of the wood and the thin edge of the Sellotape produces a sharp white line when the block is inked up

Using the Sellotape as a stencil to produce broad white lines
The block is inked up and the strips of Sellotape removed

Strawboard prints. Relief blocks made by sticking strawboard onto a sheet of paper and printing the surface of the board

Any scraps of board or card can be used for these exercises

Two exercises in cutting up a rectangle of strawboard and rearranging it to create a new form or shape

a Restriction of using only straight cuts, not throwing any piece away and containing the new arrangement within a rectangle

b Diagram of cuts made into the original rectangle

c A freer development growing away from the rectangle

a

b

c

Further prints expanding and extending a rectangle. No pieces of strawboard to be thrown away. New shapes are discovered and the white negative shapes begin to take importance. Working within certain rules and restrictions a variety of new forms and shapes can grow from the same initial rectangle

rawboard prints, exploring positive
d negative shapes

89

a

b

a and b Positive and negative strawboard prints

c The same block as in *(b)* but overprinted (in two colours) out of register to create further shapes by overlapping and leaving space in between the two shapes

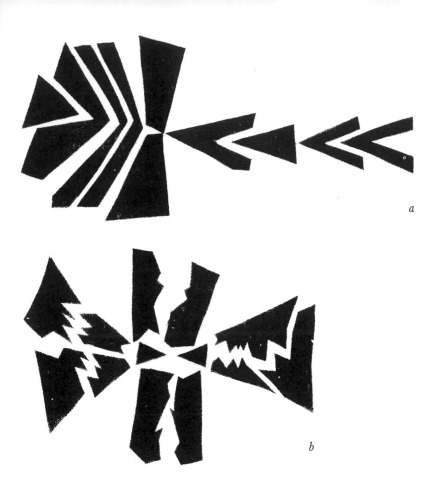

Strawboard prints

Simple expressive exercises, endeavouring to communicate an idea with abstract shapes. An exercise in defining the visual character of a shape and organising a number of shapes in relation to each other so that a given idea is expressed

Fairly thick strawboard used, forcing a solution to be found in broad abstract shapes rather than through the 'illustrated incident' (e.g. express 'falling' with a picture of a man tumbling downstairs)

a and b Collision

c, d and e Explosion

92

Further expressive exercises concerned with the idea of 'falling'

Printed paper shapes in three colours

The cut shapes are not stuck down but are inked up, placed on the paper and then printed
The cut out should be placed on a rolled up slab of ink so that it is held in place while inked. It is then lifted and placed on a sheet of paper ready for printing. The paper strengthens as the ink dries and soaks in and such shapes can therefore be used many times

a Achieving a design of white lines on [black]
by moving cut strawboard shapes close tog[ether]

b Strawboard print—Fire

a

b

Paper print

Cut out pieces of paper are stuck down onto a sheet of paper and the whole (background sheet and image) inked up and printed. The paper must be stuck down firmly or it will lift off with the roller. The ink must be allowed to soak into the paper before a good print is obtained

The white edges left by the roller give definition as does the contrast in surface of paper
This example is an exercise in extending a rectangle of paper by cutting and folding out from the centre, imposing the rule that each piece cut out must remain in contact with the preceding shape

Extended paper prints

A process in which a basic shape grows and take on another, more complex, nature

a Developed from a circle and square

b Developed from an irregular form

c and e Developed from a square

d Developed from a parallelogram

Extended paper print working from a square

Extended paper print wiping some ink away to form grey spaces

c Expanded paper cut print

d Paper print. Pieces cut from sheet of paper folded back and stuck down, whole sheet then printed

a

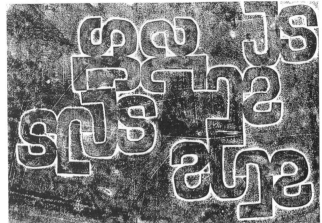

c

b

Exercises for sticking cut out paper shapes onto paper. Each print made from a given number of eight identical units

a Building an interesting new image using the most simple shape as the single unit

b and c Exercises in shape using cut paper letter forms

d A good example showing the new shapes created in between the printed shapes. The eight units losing their individual identity in place of the new larger shape

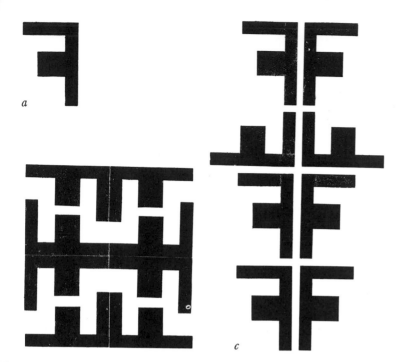

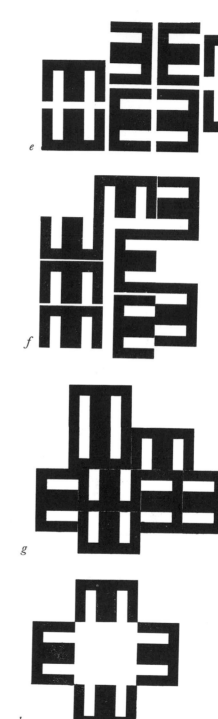

Prints made from discovered scrap metal shapes,
transformer plates
Series of exercises composing visual elements and
building shapes with a given number of identical
units

Printing unit used for *(b)* and *(c)*

A print using eight of the units. The unit loses its
identity and new shapes are formed by the white
spaces on the black

The units printed in pairs

Printing unit used for *(e) (f) (g)* and *(h)*

and f Compositions with eight units

Exercise in which the unit loses its identity com-
pletely within the new collective form

Exercise using four units in which the centre
white shape becomes dominant—ambiguous positive negative shape

6   Further experiments and direct methods

Following the series of exercises in which specific materials were explored this final section shows an attempt to find freer methods of creating printed images. These are direct methods of drawing which can produce a print without a press and without any process of sticking down or cutting out being employed.

The method of working, cutting and gouging out or sticking material down, can become so complex that it overrides the primary purpose of expressing an idea.

The examples shown consist mainly of blocks made by direct drawing with any substance that will remain in relief when dry.

Plaster of Paris, Polyfilla, Alabastine and Polyvinyl acetates can all be used. A drawing is made onto a board and the actual drawing marks are printed when the surface has dried. Such materials can be applied with a brush and the surface worked into while it is drying.

Drawings for printing can also be made with glues and pastes which, if thick enough, will create a printing surface. Whilst these dry, as with other materials, they can be pressed into or scratched through.

Relief etching is another direct method of print making which is explored in this section. The drawing is made direct onto any scrap of clean metal with a greasy substance that will resist acid.

The clear parts are etched away to form a relief block and this simple form of etching can well be done with very little material and certainly without a press.

In a relief etching on metal the basic difference from other methods is that the lower parts, or non-printing areas, can be etched away with acid rather than cut away by hand as with softer materials.

The image to be printed is drawn onto a clean plate (usually zinc) with any acid resisting substance, a greasy crayon or painted on with a greasy acid resisting varnish or shellac. The back of the plate is then covered with a resist to protect it from acid (usually a mild solution of nitric acid). The parts of the plate not protected by the greasy drawing are bitten away and lowered leaving the drawn parts untouched on the surface. After biting, the plate is washed and the varnish and grease removed with turpentine, leaving the plate ready to be inked up and printed in the same way as all other relief blocks. This method of producing a relief etching is very direct, the drawing being quite free on the plate and the acid in fact cutting the block and creating the surface.

This section also includes some monotypes. This is a direct transfer method of working in which the drawing is made onto an inked-up slab and transferred to paper while still wet. For each print the slab on which the drawing is being done must be replenished with ink, so it is not practicable to obtain two or more identical prints. However, it has many possibilities as a direct quick method and whenever a slab of ink has been used one should always be encouraged to experiment with monotypes on it before it is cleaned away.

a

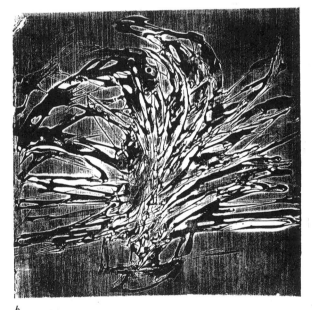

b

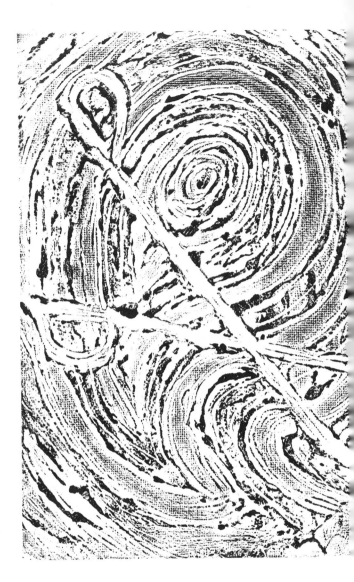

a Plaster of Paris flower painted onto a piece of board, inked up and printed when dry

b Impact glue squeezed directly onto board from the tube. Very fine ridges of glue have printed quite clearly. An immediate way of making a printed image

c Polyfilla (a type of plaster) applied thickly onto the reverse side of hardboard and drawn into while still wet with the end of brush and a matchstick

Impact glue squeezed and dribbled directly onto
board from tube

Plaster and Polyfilla print

b

Relief etchings

a Drawn mainly with greasy crayon

b Combination of free crayon drawing on plate, flat areas of stopping out varnish and areas where the varnish has been scratched through

c Experiment with various textures on a zinc plate
Fairly fine drawing with acid resisting varnish
Scratching through a painted area of varnish
Greasy crayon and sponge texture

c

a

b

c

d

Relief etchings

a Freely painted relief etching by an 8-year-old

b 'Owl' by a 10-year-old

c and d Experiments where the plate has been coated with a protective layer of varnish and then scratched through to expose the plate to the acid. The metal does not have to be scratched, only the acid resisting layer of varnish removed

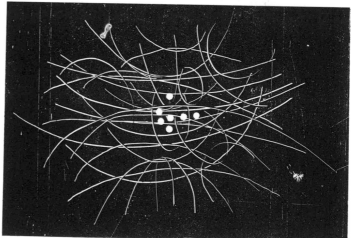

Monotype (a method of printing by which only one identical copy can be taken)

Finely drawn lines scratched into ink slab. Small circles of paper (from a hole punching machine) dropped onto the inked plate before printing

Simple torn paper monotype
drawing into inked up slab. Torn paper shapes placed on ink slab to act as a mask when the printing paper is pressed onto the ink

Monotype taken while cleaning up the ink slab and
roller. Ink slab washed with turpentine. Printing
roller run over the slab leaving textural marks.
Paper layed onto the slab and a print taken

Monotype drawn with finger on wet ink slab

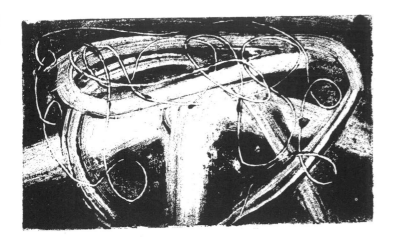

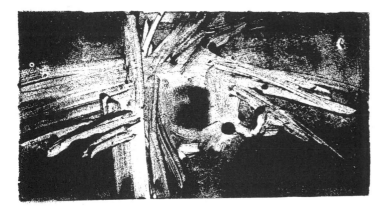

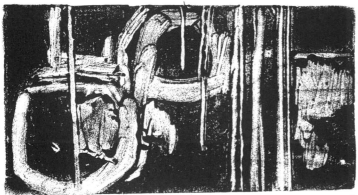

a Three monotypes
Wet ink drawn into with pencil and ball point,
finger, rag and piece of stick

b Monotype drawn with palette knife
Scratched lines combined with scraped areas

a

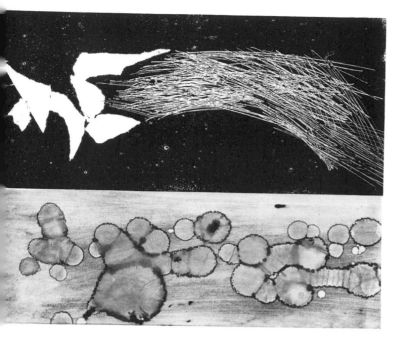

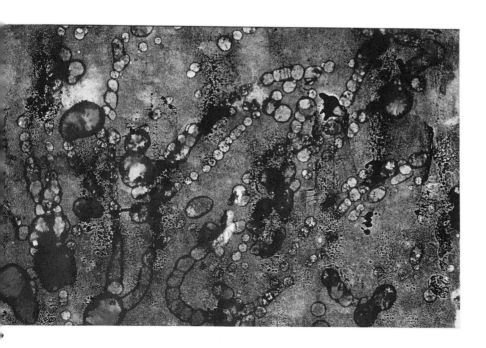

a Monotype combining fine scratched lines, torn paper shapes, and turpentine sprinkled over wiped area of plate

b Turpentine sprinkled over ink slab and paper pressed on it before it spreads

7   Practical points - Relief printing without a press

INKING UP THE BLOCK

A printing roller is used to distribute the ink evenly over the surface of the block. An even film is required so the ink is first rolled out on a slab or plate: a sheet of hardboard, metal or glass is suitable. Having worked the ink into an even consistency it is rolled over the block, the block having first been brushed clean. If a hard roller is used ink will only be placed on the very top layers of the block, but if a softer roller is employed the ink can be pushed into the lower sections of the block as well. Once it is seen what a range of different rollers can achieve the inking of the block can be controlled to suit the individual needs.

PRINTING—PRESSING THE PAPER ONTO THE BLOCK

Having completed the inking thoroughly the paper is then placed over the block and pressed onto it. A clean hard or soft roller can be used to press the paper onto the inked image, but it can also be burnished with the handle of a tool or bone folder, rubbed over with a pad of rag, or even walked over, which is very effective for large areas.

Without a press the pressure is more adaptable. Some areas can be pressed more firmly than others and the paper can be pushed into various lower parts of the block.

The amount of ink transferred from block to paper depends on the pressure and the method of printing. If the block is inked with a hard roller only the very top layers are charged with ink, if a soft roller is used ink can be pushed into some of the lower areas. Similarly in pressing the paper onto the block, if a hard roller is used to press the paper or a sheet or board placed over the paper only the upper ridges will be printed and the paper not pushed down into the block. But if a soft roller is used or the paper walked over or pressed with the hand or pad of soft rag it will be pushed down into the block and in this way, not only can the type of print be controlled, but the whole depth of the block can be used.

OFFSET PRINTING

Another simple way of taking a print without a press is by offsetting the image from the printing block to a clean roller and from the roller to a sheet of paper.

The block is inked up and a clean roller pressed over the block, this picks up the image transferring it from the block to the roller, the image is then transferred (or offset) from the roller to the paper or surface to be printed on.

This is extremely useful for detailed or fine work (the printing of leaves, feathers or a fine texture). Little pressure is needed so there is no chance of the image moving and smudging. One is limited by the size of rollers but if these are available it is one of the best and most direct ways of printing. With this method it is also possible to transfer the image onto a three-dimensional form.

REGISTRATION AND KEEPING PRINTS CLEAN

If the paper has to be registered back onto the block for a second colour printing the important thing is that the block is in the same position in relation to the edge of the paper for each printing. To do this the paper must be first trimmed to size with one corner a right angle.

A register board (a sheet of hardboard) is used with a raised 'lay' ridge along one corner. The position of the block is established and marked on the register board and kept exactly in this position for each printing, so that the block is always constant in relation to the edge of the register board. The edge of the paper is laid up to the corner ridge of the board and lowered onto the block. If the paper goes exactly into the corner lay and the position of the block is constant each colour will register accurately.

Care should be taken to keep the prints clean and after the block has been inked up the surrounds should be wiped or a clean piece of paper placed under the block so that no ink is smudged onto the margin of the print. When printing, care should be taken to avoid getting dirty finger marks over the printing paper. The print can best be held with a small piece of folded paper, called *mittens*, in the hand which will protect the margins of the paper.

When drying prints it is best to either place them in a drying rack or hang them from a line to ensure that they do not stick together or get damaged. Racks can be easily made and those made with clothes pegs or paper clips and string can be quite adequate.

Ink being rolled out onto a metal plate to obtain an even film which can be transferred to the surface of the block

Any flat non absorbent surface such as metal, glass, sized hardboard, old litho stones, is suitable for rolling out the ink

The clean margin left around the ink avoids the roller handle getting dirty if it is put down

Inking up the block

The inked block on a simple register board

This board has a raised strip of wood around two sides

This forms an edge or 'lay', up to which one corner of the paper to be printed on can be placed

Two strips of brown sticky paper mark the position where the block is to be placed. The position of the block in relation to the edge of the paper is therefore constant and accurate registration is obtained

The paper being placed onto the block
The block is in position against the brown sticky paper
The printing paper is first placed carefully up to the corner edge and then lowered onto the inked block

Printing the block by pressing with a clean roller
In this case a hard roller which will lift the ink only from the very top surface
One hand holds the paper still on the block

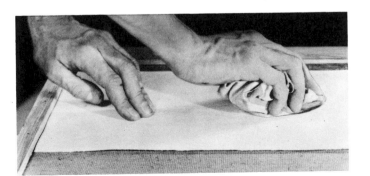

Pressing the paper with a soft rag
Printing with a soft material can be very useful when the block has a variety of depths and the paper needs to be pushed down into the lower areas
Again the free hand holds the paper to ensure it does not move

When the print is taken the paper is lifted carefully from the block
Folded pieces of paper can be used to handle the print to avoid dirty finger marks

Simple drying rack
Wooden battens and ordinary clothes pegs suspended from the wall